I0414544

SHORN SHARER

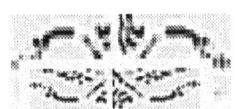

MITCHELL ALEXANDER JACKSON

© 2002 by Mitchell Alexander Jackson. All rights reserved.

No part of this book may be reproduced, stored in a retrieval
system, or transmitted by any means, electronic,
mechanical, photocopying, recording, or otherwise, without
written permission from the author.

ISBN: 0-7596-9861-9 (e-book)
ISBN: 0-7596-9862-7 (Paperback)
ISBN: 1-4033-3581-8 (Dustjacket)

This book is printed on acid free paper.

1stBooks - rev. 06/13/02

For my only other—Willie Mae
...mother

Thank you's

A heartfelt *Thank you* is extended to the research team at *Sheridan County Fulmer Public Library* for the timely facts presented within these pages—necessities that help to solidify the issues offered for discourse.

Also, a special *Thank you* is given to Research Librarian Mr. Lynn N. Friesner for his personal patience during the fruition of these pages.

TABLE OF CONTENTS

INTRODUCTION

I. THE WORD

II. IN THE WAY OF LOVE

III. THE WORD REVISITED

IV. IN THE FAMILY WAY

V. END POINT

VI. A BRIEF REGARD

VII. END NOTE

NOTE: At the publishing of this book, further thoughts on the theme presented herein may be engaged at the SHORN SHARER (...sharing an American thought) web pages. Go to http//www.geocities.com/thanqu.

INTRODUCTION

*T*he Christian heart of America, even to present day, couches *true* intent behind a "mask" of dull rhetoric and bias practices. This duplicitous image, however, can not conceal the reality that the Black soul is a marginal member of the *American tribe*, that collective people whose main culture continues to systematically deny full participation of "rights" and "privileges" to the Black segment of its population.

Why must America persist on holding onto a corrupted, manufactured representation of the dark soul?

We sons of Kanakht are entrusted with the task of "unmasking" all affronts and harmful pretensions against a suppressed people. Thus, is it our *obligation to* call into question such practices. Corrupt representations of America's Black population serves only to hamper the installation of true equality for this group of America's people. Too often was America's "promise" given. Too often was it rescinded. The *Word*, on the other hand, held out a promise non retractable, one that did not fail to nurture the hopes of this medley of Black souls, allowing the many shades of secreted aspirations to flourish within each dark bosom. Thus, unjust "levies" must not be allowed to crush the budding of tender hopes—thereby corrupting the earnest representation of the dark soul.

This maligned soul holds onto a promise of the *Word* that "grew" out of the Ancient World during times of antiquity. In that distant world are there two brothers *remembered* by God. Though God has given his promise to both theses "seeds" of Abram—the Arab and the Jew, yet are we all too eager to 'gift" total support to the latter, while insisting on a state of "non existence" fore the former, that elder brother.

Presently is there a strange parallel between America's support in the East for the one and the "lax" of support for the other, with regard to her response to souls within her own borders—in particular, souls held as being "outside" her "gifts." The dark soul in America falls within this "design." Is he "locked" into America's personally defined status of "non deserving."

Thus is this writing more of an attempt to "share" the thoughts and dreams of a Black people who has struggled under the whip, then at the side, of white America. During times of war and threat of war—not unlike within the lands of Palestine and Israel—is the Black population of America called upon, "counted on" to respond in America's defense of security and wel-being. During times of peace and "plenty," however, this same dark soul is readily "counted out."

What is "rightful," what is "deserving" is not a defining *grace* left to the whims of man, but is reserved unto God alone. However, within the purview of the will of governments to regulate and maintain its citizenry, let America do more than utter a "promise;" let her remember the "least" within her borders; let her recall these words:

> *We hold these truths to be self-evident, that all men are created equal, that they are endowed by their Creator with certain unalienable Rights, that among these are Life, Liberty and the pursuit of Happiness.*

In regard to this writing, it is hoped that, perhaps, a truer *treatment* of this maligned dark soul, herein presented, foibles in tact, may foster better understanding towards this much depreciated people. Thus, some *true* reign of freedom, perhaps, may engage even the least of America's citizenry, America's dispossessed. Might this dispossess to make confession, it shall be thus: *All joys, comforts of this great country I continually seek. With a hearty heart I breathe in, embracing—prodded on with the desire for more, acceptance, inclusion. Yet do I sleep and dream about reveling in her possibilities...my America—and hopeful to awaken to...the American Dream!*

Let there reign a rightful direction-a course *all* humanity will feel justified in embracing.

THE WORD
I

Mitchell Alexander Jackson

*In the beginning, GOD created the Heaven and the earth.
...And darkness was upon the face of the deep. And the
Spirit of God moved...*

-Genesis 1:1, 2

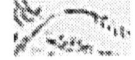

...*And* so the dark soul was "snatched up" unto *salvation*-nurtured, nestled in Christianity, which both served as "swathing clothes" and "winding cloth." From cradle to grave this Black soul was tethered to the dreams of the *American* people, was yoked by a uniquely *American* understanding of *Grace* unto "perpetual hopelessness."

But even so, this dark soul heard the *Word*-marveled in its wisdom.

So Goes The Putting Out

Should we meet
Some present day-?
Let not these words
To lip…you slay—

So you gotta get it done.
It's been hellish, grueling fun,
And your soon-to-be *orphan,*
Wrapped up in manilla—waiting—

Is given "script" and "prayer,"
A gentle kiss;
Posted. Here to there…then *there.*
(*God,* besides…only knows where!)

Persistent? You *can't* insist,
But pray a stranger…
Would take care
And shower your little *orphan* dear
With "promises" of a "word up" future—
And *waiting* meanwhile…

More waiting. A *stupor.*
Now breaking suture…
And coming all undone!

But you're the one who kicked *dear*
Out the door.
You're the one!
And you *swore* you had the mettle;
You said you knew the score.

Mitchell Alexander Jackson

Put on the kettle;
Now…pull up a chair—
There's *fun galore* to come!

Yeah,
So? You gotta,
So you go and—Get it gone…

The Christening

I

GRACE brought me here,
Shackled hand and foot;
MERCY kept me here
To breed and plant and cook...

Now, Mistress was a lady
With eyes only for Jim.
Jim-boy was my beau;
I looked after him.

Three pegs had we then.
Slow Mistress in a fit—
Often times being left at night
Alone—would titter and sit.

For Master—she knew where—
Was penned with Lolietide
—Shoo her chicks away, he would,
And put her man outside.

He'd call right out loud,
Would strip her in the light:
It tickled him to see and hear
Lo's man cry the night.

Mistress—yes, she knew—
And woman that she was—
Decided her bed she'd warm, too
—For this gave have her cause...

II

On day next, early morn—
And I laid breakfast *fine:*
Buttered biscuits! Bacon! Grits!
'Jacks and syrup! Milk and wine!

Slipped me she this note
All powdered, smelling so—
"Gal, *hurry*. The *fields*, I say!
To Jim-bo," she said. "*Go…!*"

"But, Mistress," said I then—
Mind working right to left—
"The 'seer is sure to stop me 'cause
He wants me for himself."

"No'm. Evening time is best,
When the sun has died.
Or just before the day to break
—When Master's *occupied.*

"Then Jim-boy slips right in,
And you, lying—await—
Why, Mistress! How you blush and grin!
—Well, for goodness sake!

"Well, yes'am. He is good.
But then, he is my man.
I mean, sure. M'am, he'll do
—If anybody can.

"So, keep the light real low,
And drap'ry? Keep shut down:
—No noise to wake the house at-all;
No lookers from the ground.

"Use the Master's bed,
Off in the Master's room.
No one will guess *our* plan," I said.
"And you will have your *groom!*"

Mistress, fat and giddy,
Praised me well a day,
Then made her way to "ready";
And I made out my way…

III

Jim-boy met me ready,
And swept me to the house.
"Pegs done fed and dead away;
Let's be 'cat 'n' mouse!'"

Then he grabbed me manly
—And his musk was strong!
Kissed me, then…*lord* laid me out!
—That man could do no wrong.

His arm was some hard pillow;
He snored just like a horse…
I smiled *adieu*; lifted a jug,
And went about my course…

IV

The moon winked through a peephole;
Was, lordy, dread of night-
And Lo's man sat a moanful still
Beneath his window light.

The 'seer's light was a burning
As I rapped at the door.
Just as I'd *feared*—his misses stirred
And whispered way down low:

"That you, deary Jason…?"
—Oh, my! The Master's name!
"One moment, *sweet* joy Jason!"
She called out but again.

Then the door crept open,
And her mouth flew wide;
—*My thoughts turned about, they did
And raced the other side!*

"No'm. Master's a waiting yonder.
And, child, what precious sight!
Done groomed himself with coal and oil
To black out the moon light!"

She spied the figure sitting—
Her white heart leapt and pound—
With joy, she pounced upon Lo's man,
And both rolled to the ground.

No sound, no plea came to me;
No cry awoke the air—
I smiled to think the beauty,
The *Christening* happ'ning there…!

V

I turned again to matters—
With jug in hand—slipped in

And woke the 'seer with scent and smell
Of me and jug and then—

No thought of wife nor mercy;
He wanted me and jug:
He took an age to swallow thirst,
And took me to hug.

"Meet me at the Big House;
The Master's entertained.
Tonight his room is mine," I said.
"Tonight can be your gain."

I then rushed off in swiftness.
Still he remained behind,
Till deeming the "spoil" empty.
(—Mistress was charmed on wine.)

VI

She cooed her lily love song,
And there bided her time;
And through the window crept the 'seer:
Lord, were they one in mind...

He stumbled to the bedpost
And dropped upon the bed.
With eager aid, she rent his clothes,
And this is what she said:

"True, I am no virgin;
but I am hardly used.
You will enjoy me; this I vow
—A lady un-abused."

With that, their wine and liquor
Did mingle with the air—
Just as their spirits, so did they:
Communion! Offering! Prayer!

VII

Then morning, then came evening…
All smiling! None could stop:
In sweet miraculous jubilation
Nights blazed furnace hot!

GRACE brought me here,
Shackled hand and foot;
MERCY kept me here
To breed and plant and cook…

Tim Tott

Why is you grousin', Tim Tott?
Fo' a mess of chil'en you ain't got?
Here. Take my brood, fo' hev'm',
Or take yuah pick. I got elev'm.
And one's on the way.

They'll be needin' things that sway—
Like coats and shoes—commensur'y.
And jus' ta feed'em gonna cos'.
Why, a side of pork is one meal los',
And still with two ta go.

No, Tim Tott! I say, "*no!*"
You ain't no wise ol' at sixty-fo'.
Take my eldes' fo' yauh bride.
Sixteen a give yauh a mighty fine ride.
Mark what I say be true.

Tott, I was a like bride, too.
At sixteen I was spankin' new
And Ol' Vernon had ta learn me such.
Still, *this* chile, Tott, won't take much—
A twice-tried sacrifice.

You done worked 'bout out yauh life.
Tott, high time you take a wife
And git yauself some progeny.
This young'en, she's fertile fo' seed—
Done dropped litter twice.

Can this gal *cook!* Grits *and* rice!
Yauh gol'en years, Tott? Sitt'em up nice!
No betta cook in the lower quarda,

The softes' sweet ta stinch on wada.
Ta think—your own chil'en!

Lead her, Tott. She be willin'.
Every seed calls fo' a drillin'—
Plow her garden and spike the row;
And make her fetch as you hoe,
The farmer you is.

This gal of mine is a whiz.
Sometimes the simplest is a quiz-
But "giddy," Tott, don't mean dumb.
Don'tcha want a wife what's fun?
—Or some bossy-lace?

Shame—these acres ta go ta waste.
Kudzu soon a take your place.
No prosperity in name an' lan',
Soon Tim Tott's a forgotten man—
If nothin' else.

Now Jacob's gone on. I'm on a shelf.
I'd jus' as soon wed you myself,
Since plantin' two. Tott, don'tcha fear—
Chil'en! Chil'en! Daddy's here!
Tott, Tim Tott! Where yauh go!
Honey's, that Tott done tracked the snow.

Mister Chapman

Ah, there, Mr. Chapman!
Fine day to weather here—
Some rabbit stew; a tank or two—
A soul can much forebear.
—The air, ah! Finely friend, the air!

What fine one, Mr. Chapman!
I've just this branch, myself.
Why, under cloud we spend the mile—
And we've nothing else.
—Good health, I toast you, sir. *Good health!*

—And you Mr. Chapman?
Tosh, bosh! We each our way:
You're something grand; I'm slight of hand.
Still, we say our say.
—No, stay! But hear me out, sir. Stay!

Now, there, Mr. Chapman!
A tweak is all it was—
A little smile. You know my style:
Twitter here, and there a buzz.
—Albeit, gives to pause. But cause…

Sterling Mr. Chapman!
The grandest of your band—
Topped and caned! Gold watch and chain!
And *kidded,* white gloved hand!
—Fine gentleman. Tip to toe! *Whose man?*

Good day to you, sir, Chapman!
Our yesterdays…We bear!
Still, morrows may un-smile *this* day—
God's universe still spends its fare.
Sir, take care. What load you bear. Take care…!

15

Mitchell Alexander Jackson

In The *Funnies*

"*Good old Charlie Brown*"
Was *stripped* right from my eyes.
Cathy blurbs, "A girl's gotta do,"
While Dilbert gets a rise.
B.C. is still being me;
Broom-Hilda's still quite "sweeping;"
As with Garfield, I marvel still
At Eek *and* Meek's inn-keeping.

Yet I surmise—
That Charlie Brown…*and gang*—gone…

Loved…songed—is being missed…
Beyond sunrise.

I Love My Fish On Friday

I love my fish
On Friday
And my paycheck, too.

Just to "party hardy"
Saturday all through

To Sunday dawn
And tithe
And prayer *and* song.
—*And any Tv viewer's view.*
On Monday morning
To return
To chores—broke and *blue.*

Through Tuesday? *Dido.*
And "the hump."

Swish! comes Thursday;
Gone's the slump!

'Cause, I love my fish
On Friday
And my paycheck, too.

Mitchell Alexander Jackson

IN THE WAY OF LOVE
II

Mitchell Alexander Jackson

I am black, but comely...
A bundle of myrrh is my well-beloved unto me; he shall lie
all night betwixt my breasts.

-*Song of Solomon 1:5; 1:13.*

*B*eauty is not restricted to a definition filtered through *Western* optics. Love interests and measuring weights are secreted by every culture, even that of the Black souls in *America.*

Although enticing perfumes from the likes of a Queen Kawit may be out of reach; and the exotic loveliness of a Queen Ahmose-Nefertari may be unavailable; still, nature has availed itself in such a way as to make "gifting"—a loving presentation of one's "nakedness"—much in sync with the grand design. And one dark, yearning soul can always find "beauty" in another dark "grain of sand."

My Genie Oasis

Genie…Genie…
These thoughts are of you:
So *loving* a vision,
So taunting a view.

As a cooling *oasis*
With a deep central well,
With mounds of soft bedding
To induce and *in-spell,*
To charm and entice
When in frenzied unrest—

Come, *sooth*e this hot "burning"
With your cooling caress!

So *mystic* a vision,
Enchantingly pure,
A mirage…my *oasis*…
My Genie oasis. *Untrue*…
Belied and belies-
Yet…*All* thoughts are you.

Darling Lou

Oh, my dainty, darling Lou!
Fragrant, fragile, loving Lou!
Living, learning that I do
Are done by other far greater than I—
Living, learning that I do
Falls to you: *all* reasons why!

Yet, what I do is of my best.
On followed task in soul's *unrest*:
Overtaken thoughts confess—
Aroused! You *weave*—and don't deny
My undertaken thoughts' own quest!
—Mind and soul now *must* comply!

Mysterious muse—sum soul to me,
Oh, most *sweet* rose! My *rare* lily!
Nature's nurturer…sweet caprice!
Dazzles, smiles—bedevils the sun.
Poor Nature begs *you* at a run—
"Ravish do my soul…Ah! Come!"

It's you alone who fuels my love.
Ete votre service my mute dove!
Forbidden *Amour*! Ah, the rub!
Shelved, now stilled. *Bliss*—flies "the lie:"
Heart and soul…perfect love!
Yet, next I awaken—and die…

Pen Pal

Clare—
    Lay bare
        This yellow rose—
                A *tithe* to you
                For rendered service
                And payment due
                        —Unhindered.

Smiles—
    Hope towers
        And joys untold
                You gave—and yes,
                Calm for the morn…
                Night—*blissful* rest
                        —How splendid!

Miles—
    Lone hours…
        With all else spent,
                In desperate times
                You grace me with
                Well chosen lines
                        —Intended.

Peace—
    Release,
        Your songs of thought…
                They serve me still;
                The debt remains
                And always will
                      —*Befriended!*

With This Thought

With this thought,
Though far away I be,
Still am I near—
Though out of touch…
Yet here I am to see
In *this* thought…
To caress your private world—
In listening ears I whisper…
Happy birthday, girl…!

Bereavement—SSC

There is a marriage in this town:
—Awed pompous ceremony
Shall wed a golden band around
Blue-eyed groom—Black bride: pledged only.
…In time his Black mistress swears
His corroded band—*her* veil of tears.

Mitchell Alexander Jackson

Adieu, My Mistress Dying

I

My mistress soon be smitten dead,
And I in mournful gaze,
View white clouds stalking overhead
To mask her in her place.

That cloud at *will* is pleased to come—
A cross made I to bear:
A hopeless vigil; Seducer's son
Strikes out in mindless fear.

And so my mistress suffer's ill
And slowly fades away;
Dark skin tolling a ghostly pale:
The white cloud bids to stay.

Mute will be the funeral song…
With white cloud overhead;
All *will* forgetting she ever belonged—
When this—*my* mistress's dead.

II

How brother heeds me not: I call;
He smiles upon my braid
And tells me that I am enthralled
By *politics* long laid.

But should *I*, as borne patient Job,
The *faith* to stay the mile
And hope this burden overload
Should last but no great while?

But should *I* follow where am led
On every word of speech
And turn about a rolling head
When struck upon the cheek?

But should *I* smile a warm return
To dire oaths…crude and glib?
And should *I* profit first to learn
The yoke abounds the crib?

Should I *succumb* to the lash,
Much as the Master had—
In mute repose—to strange and rash
Bonds my *brother* bade?

I say that I am bondsman no;
My *Father* knows my lot,
And feeds me manner sweet; to go
With bowed head I may not.

Holiday, Eh

Our *love*
Was like a holiday
Of sun
Blue sky
Band and
Parade

What more
You ask?

Mightn't
I say?
Plenty...

Now
That the holiday
Is over

What Says Big Mama

Look at Big Mama.
What does she say?
She says "hello" to the moon.

Look at Big Mama.
Is she ok?
It's just her love call in June:
    Royal Moon
    Glowing brightly
        Upon a dappled tapestry—
            Dancing, twinkling,
            Glimmering broad night
            Lays before your *loving* way.

        Oh,
        Sister Moon,
        Precious Selene,
        You've been here. And there am I.
        You couldn't deny—
        But sweetly betrothed
        Your King, Hunter, Shepard—
            Paining love *dearly* to slumber…
            Let me *my* love know—confer.

        Oh,
        Sister Moon,
        Precious Selene
        Shining majestically—*why*?
        Mind and eye
        Still keep reminding—
        Deliver me from my
            Cinderella plight:
            Bless me in your silvery night.

For I'm coarse
And
He is charming;
He's handsome
As
I'm alarming.

But
Love has drawn me
So—*like* you-
To
This one so fare.

      I'm grossly fat
And
He's too thin;
He smiles genteelly;
I just grin.

I'm in need
Of love—
One great repair!

Please—
As he is debonair…
Exudes *savoir faire,*
Make me his *silvery* dream
Beyond compare.

      He is the *font*
Of nonchalance—
In granting me *this* deed;
Charm…seed.
Please, sweet Selene,
Make me

His *Eve.*
All
Our love,
Sweet Royal Moon!
Dear sister—
Yes! Can be! Can be...*if only*—

Look at Big Mama.
What does she hear?
She hears "hopeless" from the moon.

Look at Big Mama.
Is she ok?
        She is weeping...out of tune:
        So long Moon.
        Good-bye, *romance.*
                Love's glow's gone—
                Shut down the dance.

Mitchell Alexander Jackson

Rhythm 'N' Lovin'

I got the beat
I'm soundin' *sweet*
Can make you shimmy
—Make you *pop* your feet!

I swing it high
Then sound it low
Let me *trip* your *tootie*
—Make you *go, go, go*!

Scat Jazz Lover

If you say you
Need a lover
'*Cause* you're in a jam.
Say, if you need a lover,
I say, baby, I'm your man!

Say you in need?
Need love no other;
I'm "Lover on demand."
Jelly, jam—hey!
Pound or gram!
—Call me, baby. Here I am.

If you say you
Need a lover,
I'm, well, who I am.
Say, if you need a lover—
Say jelly, or just say jam!

You needn't fear.
Fear no recover,
I'm "Lover on demand."
Jelly, jam—hey!
Pound or gram!
—Call me, baby. I'm your man.

Hey!
Scat, do-wat
De-be-dat

Shat, dab
Do-be-de

Wah, do-waw
Bar, do-waw—
Schoo-be, doo-be
Shat; do-we-eeeee!

If you say you
Need a lover—
Like hours on the strand…?
Say you need a lover
True—'cause baby, here I am!

Yes, we can!
Said Sammy *D*—
Needing
"Loving on demand"?
Jelly, jam—hey!
Pound or gram!
—Call me, baby, here I am.
'Cause I'm your man…!

I say…
Jelly, jam—hey!
Pound or gram!
—Just call me, baby, here I am!
Schoo-be, do-be
shat, do-we-eeeee!

THE WORD REVISITED
III

Mitchell Alexander Jackson

Bless the Lord, O my soul...God, thou art very
great...clothed with honour and majesty.
Keep me as the apple of the eye, hide me under the shadow
of thy wings...

-Psalm 104:1; 17:8.

*T*oo easily a culture is rendered "myopic" as to its understanding with the *Creator*. Most common is it for a culture to wrap its own "spiritual expressions" within the guise of a relational oneness with the *Supreme Being*, placing itself uniquely-as *chosen out* from amongst the multitude. To do so, thus becoming shortsighted, allows for the negating or ignoring completely the importance of the honor of *God* and *His* spiritual "stirrings" amongst various cultures—and these cultures' various religious canons and beliefs.

When a dark soul pronounces that he has "been to the mountain top," one can only rejoice-knowing that spiritual growth of *all* cultures are of unique concern to *God*.

Dark Wonder

Floating *long*...on seas of green:
Capping ever souse...and foam,
Regent Boreas winds my sail—
Steering windward...home...

Mitchell Alexander Jackson

The Grooming

Saw a Mistress
Combing her hair today—
Sparkling…flowing…
As the Milky Way,
Undulating—
Tinctured by degree;
And as *dark*
As "*The Mystery.*"

Head in motion;
Hairs *falling* away
Caught the combing—
Every sweep and sway
Teasing the beater;
Stroke on stroke *in play*
—Just to see her!
—*And my soul gave way…*

Caressing favors fell.
Each stroke bore,
Touching my soul-string—
And to its very core…
—So played the beater,
Coursing lengthy thread,
Sparkling there the *wonder*—
Ah! My soul being fed!

With even Boreas
Winding sail at journey's end,
Would still my sad soul fail—
For my life is founding
To the night;
But her gentle grooming

Speaks new light:

Consider this *dark* course
—"*The Mystery*"—
As uncertain life
Was meant to be,
In the darkest hour
Was meant to thrive:
Koinonia...
This deaden soul alive!

With each course and curl
My soul is *spun*!
Witnessed by the *Spirit*
Of the Son.

Quakes! Away to treasures
Realized...
God's own glory—*Christ*!
—Lo! *Paradised*!

Mitchell Alexander Jackson

The Livery

There is a *Tiger* in the Wood
—*Unloosed* upon the land.
Although he's just a whelp,
They *swear* that he's a man.
And he's *stalking* broad the "green"—
What an *awful*, cudgelled *good*!
—No strident, sportive mein…
There is a *Tiger* in the Wood.

There is a *Tiger* in the Wood
Causing havoc to the stays!
As to steer him? *Of no good.*
Such belies to "by-gone" ways!
What a "mystery" divine:
Non-evasive! Dark! *Unproved!*
Reinventing "Christian mind"—
There is a *Tiger* in the Wood.

There is a *Tiger* in the Wood
To mend the silent heart—
To *unbosom*…to explode
The Mind—What craft! The *art!*
A "rebuttal" for the *soul*…
God! Does the *Spirit* good!
—An Eucharist unfold'—
There is a *Tiger* in the Wood.

44

Affrikata

I am dying, Father…
Yes. I know, my son.
I am dying, Father…
You're not alone. The drum
    Speaks.

This world of ours collapses about us—
A *universe* disbanded;
Our vision—though our focus
Clouds-*revives* and now expands
Beyond these hapless, tendriled arms,
Beyond these spindled legs.
The *Western World* alarms, my child,
Being caught up in our dregs.

I am dying, Father…
Yes. I know, my son.
I am dying, Father…
My son, the season's come;
        Sweeps…

Years bank up, unceasing years—*un*-still.
Blessed sun: a bitter herb,
Does suck all life to kill—
Wasting the human and the herd.
The "faithful" as the "other" is
—A *Sacrifice* for Time and sun…
As camel babe, his mother is—
Just "sweeping's waste" when season's done.

I am dying, Father…
Your mother loved you so.
I am dying, Father…

Son, in love, we, too, shall go.
>   *Meets.*

Branch is broken. As the winded thread
The "knowing" *Weaver* crafts with art…
The soul is surely *spun* where led.
So, if this "dark" content our lot:
Dusk upon the hot winds blows—
We fall to shadows stretched beyond.
Fear not, "love." For *Love* it is who calls;
My son, *my all*, be not alarmed.

But I am dying, Father…
Yes. My son…be still.
But, *Father,* I am *dying*…
Embrace. Hush…!
>   *Allah's* will.

The Fisherman

Ninety miles across the sea:
An alien—*all lost*—alone...
 buoyed over wave and foam
From tropic *Cuba* by degree,
Had ventured out upon the calm
With sweet *madre*—from home towards home.

Ninety miles across the sea:
All sailed from isle toward *Paradise*;
All sailed in *faith* toward the sun:
La madre, su nino, and company,
Their joyous *el mundo* soon to come.
They sailed their star—stars in their eyes.

Ninety miles across the sea:
Madre y nino, with the few
Nearing *Paradise*—sailing in joy,
Soon realized all *not to be.*
Algarada! All a toy—
To wind and stern wave taxing true.

Ninety miles across the sea:
Cinco suns had died and shown;
Seis, since venturing upon the deep:
No port, no vessel, no entry;
Just sole *nino*—as though asleep,
Crested upon a rippling foam.

Ninety miles across the sea:
Toll of day and calmer wave,
Lone *barco, pescador* and kin
(Sparked by some *divinity*)
Broke the wave off fishing when

They trekked upon a watery grave.

Ninety miles across the sea:
Two faint hearts heaved and fell;
Four eyes loosed their pent-up tears:
What *must not* could only be.
Great their sorrow grew...and fears;
Cursed two souls *el Diablo's* hell!

Ninety miles across the sea:
Entre la espada y la pared,
The *pescador* gridded his *barco,*
Heaving prayers to Virgin *Madre,*
Praying her answer not be "no"-
Plowed crest and fold...as though led.

Ninety miles across the sea:
Four eyes *gravely* sought all round;
Two hearts stopped and stopped again—
Debris yet...and more *debris*
(As prayers and curses equally frame
Winds at dusk) beyond...beyond the sound.

Ninety miles across the sea:
Devastation—nothing more.
"Todos perdida!" kinsman wept;
Into the calm-like apathy
Of just woke wind and wave that slept
The true *pescador's barco* bore.

Ninety miles across the sea:
Devastation...misery.
"Todos perdida!" kinsman wept.
But the *pescador,* fixed was he,
And fanned aft—and forward swept;
And there! A crest! A spray at lee!

Ninety miles across the sea:
Dolphins…waving the *barco* on!
Pilot, kin revered the sight:
"Madre!" "Milagro…!" Mystery:
One lone *nino*…ringed in night;
Nestled; lifted; ringed from harm.

Ninety miles across the sea:
Pescardor cleaved the watery grave;
Kinsman looked on as lubbers do;
And dolphins trumpeted with glee
As sole *nino*—of the sailed-off few
From *Cuba's* breast—alone was saved.

Ninety miles across the sea:
And kinsman marveled the prize-
Nino's tale: being "nose" cupped
By dolphins; of *dark* hours; and he,
Pescador here who wouldn't give up…
Who now steered on toward *Paradise.*

That Girl Makes My Dreams

I can't help
Remembering…
What *had* bend…and *hadn't* been—

What a pretty thing:
She *and* me.
Could have cruised the bars—
She, *my* Venus;
I, *her* Mars. But then…

Cain't say I met Lewinsky-
More like, I *know* the girl:
"My!" To think: "How pretty!
My God, give *her* my world!"

That one who spied old Clinton—
Him with his social ways…
She became *his* good friend.
—Leaving me all a dazed.

Now my nights be lonely
And be blue the days:
I long for that girl only—
With her *social* ways.

But never mind this heartbreak.
And never mind this pain.
I'd give all just for her sake
—And praise my God again.

Just to see her *smiling.*
Oh! Just to say "Hello!"
How she makes my heart "bell" ring.
—But…I'm no Romeo.

So, I guess it's over
Before it had begun.
She prefers a "rover…"
So—I guess the best man won.

What could never be
Best the worst in me.
Yet, she makes my dreams…
My God…she makes my dreams.

Paula Zahnic Balm

Paula Zahn
Paula Zahn
You are this large world
Turning

Soul's own *atom* burning
—Paula Zahn

World at bond!
Please, respond!
Faith's dedicated
Yearning:
Disarm the ills with caring
—Paula Zahn

Man's own harms!
Sound alarms!
Touch. Remake trans-
Forming
Breathe some special learning
—Paula Zahn…

Paula Zahn
Paula Zahn
Catalyst dis-
Cerning

Speak! Heart…mind…seed stirrings…!
—Paula Zahn

O!
Cosmos' own
Soul's *atom*

—Keep…keep her spirit
Glowing…
—Paula Zahn

In your *knowing*
Paula Zahn
Keep all flowing
Paula Zahn

—Seed for sowing
Paula Zahn

Paula Zahn…
Paula Zahn…
—Seed…sowing…
Paula Zahn…

Sylvan Braun!

Sylvan Braun! Sylvan Bruan!
My world is turning backwards round!
Tell the spirits to desist.
Sway them, please—I'm at triste.
Tell the spirits to retreat—
Tell them more, I'm not for "meat!"

Give them guidance; please commence—
Don't rely on mental hints:
Verbalize! *Do* speak the *Word!*
It's as though they've never heard!
'Round and 'round as ticks the clock,
I cry: "Away! You spectral flock!

Crown woodlands! Why *here* pause?
Endear the maid who gives you cause!
I worship God—as she! And *Christ*!
Seek—worship *she* who spins advice!
No *mental* crown here summons you—
Adios! Away! *Au revoir! Adieu!*"

Sylvan Braun! Sylvan Braun!
My world is turning backwards round.
Past ill-fortunes spike my dreams—
Penalties! Passions! Twisted schemes!
—Your "gray voices" put in "play,"
Band their trawling—drive them away!
Sylvan Braun! Sylvan Braun!
Bush down your "voices" still in play!

Wondrous Lost

Oh—
Let me love tomorrow…
Be lost—*forget* today.
For the pain that seared my soul
Now fainting…fades away.
And in it's place—what wondrous loss!
No joy—all pain is fell
Of neither *hot*—
Of neither *cold*—
But of a lukewarm hell…

Oh—
Let me not bear love today.
Yoked not—but to my pain.
Lost tender years…*un-circumcised.*
—Why court the *un-insane*—?

Mitchell Alexander Jackson

Love Song

On the first night
Tears—a century of tears
Lott could not have wept more

On the second
Anxiety—and great faith
The light of Job's faith was as a worm's glow

Of the first week
Hope—such as that of Abram

—But…
Something did not happen

She did not call
Weeks—and melancholy grave
Looming o'er this merchant mis-fortuned

Struck at my soul
And withered dry my spirit
Claiming all—leaving ought my own

Cool moonlight blows

Numbs my brain
—Blasting cold fires hot—
Laying waste my spent spirit

Still thoughts do come
At times—weeping o'er my soul
With joys unfolded and patient smiles

Whispered refrain
Her eyes—twin wells of passion
Pledge in fretted rhythm her love…

No *Solomon*
Wisdom may prove false
—Or dissuade—
Will I wait!

Even ever…

Mitchell Alexander Jackson

IN THE FAMILY WAY
IV

Mitchell Alexander Jackson

For whither thou goest, I will go; and where thou lodgest, I will lodge; thy people shall be my people, and thy God my God...
All that thy say unto me I will do.

-Ruth 1:16; 3:5

*T*here is commonly held that perception "suggesting" the Black soul in *America* is void of any effective culture. The logic running—a people "reduced" into *slavery* is *valueless*—especially with the male aptly "displaced." But one does not, then, appreciate the tenacious "witnessing" of a Sojourner Truth.

The thread that has the burden of holding *any* culture together, however—of old and present-day—is the female gender. The "family unit" is defined by the "feminine" heart. And the female is the "cohesion" of the family unit. The dark feminine soul—being "estranged" from the *American* society—is, one may then surmise, not unlike the humble Ruth who steadfastly maintained "family commitment" to mother-in-law Naoni, even unto increase.

Gifting

Mothers…
>   *Love* your children:
>   Babies, born…*unborn.*

Fathers…
>   Precious beacons:
>   Gift potent
>   "Carry-ons."
>   This *blood* from water mix
>   Creates such "alloyed bronze":

Memories
>   *Fatherly worn…*
>   Pressed gems…or fully blown,
>   Lingering *treasures*
>   Of valued, timely stone.
>   *Fathers…caring. Gone…*

Blood…
>   From water *mixed.*
>   *Young memories…anon.*
>   What shall linger fixed?
>   Be it sand
>   Or stone!

Mitchell Alexander Jackson

Lullaby

Southern town
Brown baby
Sleeping in the noonday sun…

Daddy's gone.
Mama sings.
And noonday's just begun.

A bit to eat
Is still a treat—
Still shadows being swept along…

Baby sleeps—
Mama sings…
And Daddy's long, long gone.

Some Special Treat

Catch you later, sugar-sweet.
No. I can't take the time just now.
But I'll be back tomorrow, anyhow.
So, *off* me woman. Need I repeat!
Now, now, sugar, I'm still your booger,
But them tears won't help my feet.
Hush, I say. Good Pete! What now?

Please, no looking like…well, some cow.
I swear, woman, I'm all brow beat!
Sugar, I allow, I screwed up somehow.
But I love you. There. Done said it now.
Oh, Lord…! Why must man fly by his seat?
Sugar? Baby, honey? Stop that squalling.
Gone and got my skin a crawling.
So sorry, baby. Some gum? Special treat?

Now. That's my sugar. *Sweet* sugar.
You ticklish, honey? I see you smile!
Perked right up! Percolator still in style?
A smooch. Give it up for your booger.
Mm, girl, can you set my soul afire!
My soul's at that Marvin Gaye *higher!*
Baby, can you figure—*working* you booger!
Chocolate sundae. Sweet little devil you…
But these feet keep looking at that mile—
And daybreak's growing all the while.
Kiss or two—? Baby, that'll have to do!

Mitchell Alexander Jackson

Unwed Mother

Song sung.
Day done.
Baby curled and hugged.

Time tolled.
Cot cold.
Mama rocks…*unloved*…

And
Hot blue spears
Pierce her aching nights,

Rock
her longing years
—*Deprived* delights.

And son.
And Sarra Lee.
Stretch out where Mama lies.

Wee
Moon lips tickle…
As *Dark* gurgling flies!

Life's fine…

Firm hip—
Lace slip
Gentle babies fond.

Still cares.
"Favors"
"Youth-*ful*" bides *alone*…

Now
The *dying*—
Her longing piece of mind.

Still not
Forgotten—
His "*Mama, looking fine*!"

But so
—Like *love*—
Seems all but *lost* its tone.

'Cause
Her sweet William
Booked-up-is long, long gone…

Just Mama.
Baby, Sarra Lee.
—And *darkness*…coming on.

Mitchell Alexander Jackson

Little Tiny Teardrops

Oh, little tiny teardrops,
From where do you fall?

Falling from the eye
Of an orphan girl and boy
Who never had a mother
To really understand,
Who never have a father
—To make their small demands.

Just tears of solemn sorrow
From eyes whose vision blears,
With one thought of tomorrow—
To find someone who cares…

Oh, little tiny teardrops
From where do you fall?
Falling from the eye
Of an orphan girl and boy…

Oh, little tiny teardrops
From where do you fall?

Falling from the eye
Of an orphan girl and boy
Who never had a mother
To kiss and hug them tight
Who never had a father
To tuck them in at night.

A blessing for the many,
Defiance for the few
Who shed teardrops a plenty
—And love's the only cure…

Oh, little tiny teardrops
From where do you fall?

Falling from the eye
Of an orphan girl and boy
Who never had a mother
To squeeze with great delight,
Who never had a father
To make their small world right.

Just tears of solemn sorrow
—That sad and pensive stare—
Wishing a tomorrow.
Would anybody care…?

Mitchell Alexander Jackson

The Purple Cat 'o Lac

I am the *Purple Cat' o Lac*
And here's a well known fact.
I *do* the very *normal* things
Us *Cat' o Lacs* do.

I can walk with my nose
And sing through my toes,
Swim the *Great Blue Breeze*—
Just to name a few.

Fessing up, I'm no cat special.
Hate to say, yeah—*rehearsal*,
When learning how to do
Without regrets.

Still—when *Lac Cats* roam?
Why, foreign lands are just like home—
Moaning *Zero*! *Counting* numbers!
And dancing the alphabet!

Oooo! Zero, don't you know.
Before that lonesome *One,* it comes.
Unless it's left behind.

Next, scooting up is *Two*—
A-tipping Saint Nick right down the flu...
'Cause baby *Three* is waiting—snuggled up fine.

Now knocking at the door
And wanting in is *Four*. Shakes alive!
Why, numbers do abide!

Goodness! Up rocks *Five!*
And *lickety-split* comes *Six*—
Rolling up with his bag of tricks!

But not to worry!
Old number *Seven* is in *no* hurry.
That numeral is out to hook a date—

Making *Eight* just a little bit late…
So poor, poor *Nine*
Never shows up on time!

And *Oooo!* My friend,
Here he comes, that *Zero* comes again!
If I didn't better know, I'd call it a trend.

Numbers! Digits!
Always counting themselves *in*—
Coming and going, going and *always* coming!

Yes, I'm the *Purple Cat' o Lac.*
Just what you think of that
Is up to you. *Suits me, too.*

I'm no smarter than my brother
Or no purple any other *Cat' o Lac.*
Just take it as a fact.

Sure. I can dance an airy "*A*"
—But bully "*B*" just crowds my way,
Chases me tripping up a fur tree—
On an angry cyan "*C*".

So, I sit and fish a while.
First, a nibble makes smile,
As I reel in that dancing "*D*"!
—And rejoicing "*E*" eee-eagerly.

No? If you say so.

Okay. Got a little carried away
Is all. No tears all day. Okay?
Give us another try? Can we?
I'll share just what we *Lac Cats* see…!

"*F*" I dance? And I *can* dance.
Then "*G*" ee, I can, I can *romance*
Miss *Cat' o "H."* She curtsies. And "*I*,"
To waltzing, *woo* her, by-the-by.

First, we "*J*" dance a little while;
"*K*" Promenade with a *personable* style!
Then *loop d' loop* the "*L*", you know?
Next, we "circle left" about the floor!

…Getting an "*M*" mm with a sashay "*N*,"
While giving my "Miss" a lightning grin!
Dipping her lightly? She says "*O*" oo…
Then it's a *whirl* about the floor!

Miss would fain to faint, just so,
While watching our "*P*" s and" *Q*" s—we go!
"*Heel* and *toe*." Now our big *finale*—
Stepping off—"*R*," "*S*," "*T*," "*U*," "*V*."
Wheeee!

This *Cat' o Lac* is now home free!
I swing my Miss—one, two, three—
Four to go. Don't you agree? Then it's the *end* of me!
Well, here we go! "*W*," "*X*," "*Y*," and "*Z*" zzzz!

Something Just Don't Seem Too Right

You had a fight with your turtledove.
Know her to be your one true love
And try to tell her over again—and more.
From a hard day's work, you open the door.
What to greet you on your living room floor,
On a white bear rug, is your darling wife,
A bottle of ale to pass the night—
And some strange guy having the time of his life!

And you try—again and again,
You try to comprehend—
Something about this set-up
Just don't seem right…

She hadn't heard a word you said.
The two of them prepare for bed—
—*You*? The back porch and your *good* night!

Sleepless nights as the days go on.
Knowing she's in another's arms.
A hundred times and, "She's not in!"
He makes *his* point—so *you* call again.
Though you don't understand, you'd like to make amends.

What to greet you at your own front door
Is that strange guy—and what is more
He's in your "PJ's" and throwing kisses
To your wife on the floor.
—You're out of the door nodding your "Good night."

And all this while close to half your check
Is going to pay for that stranger's debt—
Clothes and shoes, a permanent set of curls.

The other half—they're living up whirls.
—You're barely surviving night-outs at the grills.
Financially, you're too hard pressed.
Your social life's "Joe's Bar's" tv set.
This whole rigamarole is leading to a pauper's death.

And you try again—and a gain.
You try to comprehend—
Something about this set-up just don't seem right…
You call—and *she* calls you dirt and soot
And tells you to please kiss her butt—
And you smile…at the *new* dawn's Coming light!

You smile because she talked to you.
You smile…because she listened, too.
—The reason for thinking everything will be all right—?

Well, when she *said* to kiss her butt,
You felt a change, then, in your luck-
For the girl said *please*—
Sure 'nough, a brand new lease on life!
You tried—now you understand
And now know that you're her man
—Just wait a while. And everything will be all right!

Can't Nix The Mix

My dearest wants me to real quick
    To put away my music
    For some "nine-to-five."

Just pack away my *freedom side*
    For some boss-ass jive—
    Pack away my *believin'.*

I'm gonna make it yet!
    Got the sound and lingo—
    Just need a bit more sweat.

That woman's packed for Georgia.
Me—! I'm bound for Tennessee.

Mitchell Alexander Jackson

The Promise

You promised me a poem *always*
Of long legs and *leading* eyes
And tones of *sweetness*
Gathered up in taffy-pulling
Thralls—

Of *perfumed* beds
And sheets sweaty
With cries!
Of heated *bliss!*

All—balled and wrapped!
Arms and legs recruiting;
Kissing *all…!*

But now—
Long passed the ringing
Of *razed* passions—
While in age I lie
Contented.
In calm *Remunerations…*
Pillowing your head.

Yet—you said,
Had *promised…*
Though contented. I abide—
Still…I feel *sweet-love* denied.

A Slice Of Heaven

I'm on this *other* side of heaven.
But—I'll give it one more try.
Joy! And all! And all in living!
     Now, I'm living just "the *lie*."

Through the years, I've been giving
All those years *in love*—gone by.
She's *now* alone…no longer willing—
     Here's some *Heaven*—"In your eye!"

You, oh, yes, may have guessed
I swill a drink upon a time.
In turn, I'm just a bloody mess:
     This side of heaven ain't for the blind.

Mitchell Alexander Jackson

END POINT
V

Mitchell Alexander Jackson

The thief cometh not, but for to steal, and to kill, and to destroy...

—*John 10:10*

*O*nce again, it is commonly held-believed—that the Black soul in *America* is void of any effective "culture," there being so many a dark soul in prisons. To suggest there is "persuasion" abounding from all camps is a given. Undue destructive influences have worked well to help "populate" his prison number. Not all Black folk are deserving of stripes.

Perhaps, no culture better understands diversity as well as *America's* dark culture. Aside from the female Moseses—the likes of a Harriett Tubman, male titans shadow the heavens in *American* history.

Two such polemic personalities were then the youthful William Edward Burghardt Du Bois and the venerable Booker Taliaferro Washington. Both, desiring for the dark race the same end, endlessly expounded his own preference for the long-sought after *prize* held in common-*true equality*—often in public disputes, but never losing sight of "the common good."

But the dark soul has experienced, as well, his own brand of Benedict Arnolds. Such Black folk, understanding little...and caring less for "the common good," sets *will* toward personal profit, gain. To attempt to number them would realize a "fruitless" effort. But each, to the head-affirms in "speech" and "deeds" an *ill* concern with respect to *America's* Black population. Their response is as if to assert that what's good for *America* is of no consequence to the dark, "*christened*" soul.

Of Precedence

And now—you and your misses, on your way
To dreams *untended* and to hopes *anew*,
These "virgin territories"—as shall ensue
On "turning the reins over," as they say…
As *democratic process* deems okay.
When *stepping off,* departing from the "few"—
That *august* three-tier ruling retinue—
"Hail and farewell"—yours was the one bright ray!

Go knowing that the sun has not yet set:
You "ministered" with an even hand;
Your note in history shall *forever* stand:
Melodic strains of grace—such sweet fiet!

Yes, *dullards* pray that yours was just a lark;
But we who "know" say you have hit the mark!

Mitchell Alexander Jackson

The Consolation Prize

I can understand an *Indian*
Becoming an Indian chief;
Or a *Washington*…a president,
With his frills and perfumed scent;
Or his opposite: a *Lincoln*—
Whose brow had *borne* the grief…

But…I've been thinkin',
And with *no* great relief:
    What Black man
    With Democratic sand
    Dares to prize himself
    A Republican…?

Gentle Despair

There is no "hatred" in the *land*.
Just a steel of mights
That bind the mind to profit poor
And stone the "common rights."

And no "injustice" to be found.
Just a heavy hand.
That squeezes *loving* from the mold
And sears the naive man.

But what there is—in *clouds*—obeys
The savagery spent,
That suffocates with aspic pains
The *good*, the *innocent*.

There is no "malice" in the *world*.
Just a purple rose
Whose thorns do rip the tender heart
And slay the gentle soul.

Mitchell Alexander Jackson

Makin' A Million

Gotta make a million.
When is that a crime—?
Till then, she ain't forgivin'.
    Buddy—can you spare a dime?

Gonna make a million
With my next release.
Till then, are you sparin,'
    Buddy—say…a two-bit piece?

Gettin' me that million
For the world and her to see!
Till then…bread I'm breakin,'
    Buddy…with hard misery.

Goin' for that million.
So, when is it a crime…
Till then, I'm barely livin'.
    Buddy—can you spare a dime?

The Man Said

The man said, "*Hell…!*"
And I agree.
What the hell's come over me?

Then was I told.
But *now* I know—
I've a long, long ways to go.

I should have heard
When was I told.
Guess it just *nohow* took hold.

Old circumstance
Has whipped its tail;
Don't know some-wise if I'll prevail.

But *if* I do
—Say that I stand—
Won't be buying no plot of land—

Nor fancy car;
No trendy boat—
This life done got me…by the throat!

Nor big, old house;
No grand, high job:
I'll leave the mob, *hell!* To the mob!

And no parade;
No primal fun—
I know how *swings* the pendulum.

Without it all,
I guess you'd frown,
"*What kind of life's that, anyhow*?

"*Just do the work,
By steps degree…
And sure on sure you will succeed.*

"*Reward!*" you say,
"*All heaven-sent!*"
—But this I know *ain't* Parliament.

What *God* provides
Don't always stay—
'Cause with man's law *"good"* always pay.

Gone tomorrow.
Ain't here today—
Grace and *fortune*…both "pressed" away:

Heavy *envy*
And trumped up "cause"
Harry *reason* with vicious claws.

What laws, when fail
To "rope-a-dope,"
Malice *all bloody* the bones of *Hope.*

Bruise to murder—
Another degree.
Don't recognize *no* company.

Now, well I know
What I'm to do:
Gotta live a life led by the few.

Forget what power;
Forget what pride:
Follow the course of the *Neap Tide*.

Life's sometimes charmed;
Life's sometimes hard:
Sometimes man's life *forget* the *God.*

That *God* is *God*...
And man's *just* man—
"This something" *all* must understand!

What you live,
How you endure
Ain't *sure remedy* for no "cure."

If malice, *no*—
Still ain't no draw:
Life's got what's called the "Murphy Law."

Then, there is "Peter"
What takes a toll—
Another *God-forsaken* principle!

Here man-mute *God*—
Now trumped up card...
Make life what's living *cursed* hard!

In living life,
Don't be surprised
If, all in all, you are despised—

Broken...bleeding
—As left for dead:
Some serpent who's done *bruised* your head!

When nothing's left
But wide the grave,
Now is no time you need "behave";

Don't scream no more,
Don't kick, don't bite—
Life *ain't* about making "wrongs" right.

Now, listen close,
and closer still—
This what you do: *exert your will.*

Be moderate—
Now, this you do:
To *form* and *course*, you keep. "Hold true."

Don't plow too wide;
Don't spade too low:
Straight and narrow what's stay the row.

Don't live so high;
Don't love so deep:
Some things in life-? It just don't keep.

And when life's done,
Such is the pot:
A "*dead man's*" hand is all you got.

No thing of gain
Is *no* thing kept.
They tell me even *Christ Jesus* wept.

Yeah, man cried, "*Hell*!"
'Cause as it go,
Gotta *live* your life outside the "know."

Beyond Clinton

    I won't be knowing,
Baby. I'm no
Psychologist—
No "feel-good" pill I want to know,
No *Raganomic* wish—
    All life been "trickle down," Lord only knows…
    Nothing in this place is sound.

You an' me?
Still without. For *good* or *ill*—
Pound for pound…I see no cause to shout.
No *Jubilee* on the horizon.
And no *Saint John* a coming baptizing.
    No, Baby…
    I won't be knowing…

Mitchell Alexander Jackson

A BRIEF REGARD
VI

Mitchell Alexander Jackson

*T*he wonder of a people can not exist outside the *Mind of God*. The magnificence of a culture has less left to doubt about itself when the "active nature" of God moves against the broad ways of institutional bigotries, prejudices, and neglect. Every earthly culture has experienced the benevolence of God's "insistence"—proving a Godly integrity—a must by a *Creator* towards "affirming" his creation.

To extricate "culture" from "history" or "history" from an ever-present God is an impossibility. Be aware that no "secreted" act goes without a "witness"; no open aggression goes without a diminishing of that communal body. And, furthermore, towards all does the *Will*...the *Love* of God preserve.

The following poems are especially here noted, evidentially referencing that special relationship between Creator and the created; between the created and like creation.

Of Precedence

With day falling upon day, the *ideal* of the *American* dream appears to not be held  *en masse* for all America's inhabitants—including her citizenry. For the "attitude" that would "call itself fourth" to rule a country and a people has selected to make arbitrary such important pillars as *Freedom, Justice,* and *Obligation* in this—our—society. The *Biblical* scholar may recall the warning that *the thief comes but the steal...kill...destroy.*

Presently, with the mantles of this new regime being used to yoke the patient and to exacerbate the hopeful, many Americans grew to appreciate all the more the former administration and its leadership. Therefore, to former President Clinton and his wife, do I humbly offer a personal "thanks" to what must now be a long line of grateful acknowledgments. Under Mr. Clinton's Presidency was there prosperity; presently is there confusion and uncertainty. The "whisper" from certain quarters suggesting that Mr. Clinton "stole" former President Bushe's Whitehouse does not ascribe to the American ideal. Neither may it be supposed as a legitimate thought; but if so, if one may infer, then it can only be said that the world has turned upside down.

The Livery

Perhaps, that traditional spirit is "on the move"—is again making its *presence*.
The "Tiger In The Wood" poem presented itself "fully blown" during *la entre* of one *Tiger Woods*...a young man professing the lineage of several cultures.

I rejoiced when I realized the importance of this message. Still, how genuine is the poem? Poetics is art. How much of the poem is crafted..."contrived?"

Having waken that morning to the thought with the account of young Mr. Woods' exceptional round of golf over the radio, at one point I did address the poem. I questioned while, watching the poem "spill" unto the page. For I had become confounded by this one element in the poem. In short, I challenged its "integrity." *"Unproved."* This was the area of contention. How could this be? In order to get where he did, surely was he tested. I decided that I "misunderstood." Shortly after, I "corrected" the "fault" with the word *"Proved."*

Later, having "wrestled" with this for some time, I came to realize that the fault was mine. My understanding had I limited to the "experiential." The poem, more expansive, appears to speak beyond the talents of the youthful Tiger Woods...and beyond the physical. It seems to speak of an "engaging"..."insistent" Power—Creator—beyond the veil of man's own knowing...

Perhaps there's a message on the "horizon"? Let us as Americans consciously hearken to the

Spirit of thanks and giving—*embracing* "tolerance" and "inclusiveness."

The Fisherman

Here in America—the *United States*—this  Republic, we are ever thrusting Democracy and "Freedom" upon those beyond our reach. Others *within* our borders, however, we smother with *"love failing."*

Not long past, a Cuban youth was "fished" from the sea. His survival was nothing less than miraculous. Upon these shores was he subjected to politics uniquely American. A country valuing *"family unity"* and *"rule-of-law"* was prepared to play politics with the life of one so desperately plucked up, one so tenderly immature—but five years of age—*yet still so near the cradle.*

The Hispanic community, however, reverberated concerning the rescue on a level beyond...above the politics that permitted this incident. Their collective response was one of religious connotations. "Religion" *and* "culture" had elevated the near tragic into the "sublime." Thus, where our politicians saw "political leverage," the Hispanic community saw the "Divine."

My account of little Elian Gonzales "dark hours" upon the waves are not merely a poetic thought, but it's an attempt to record what seems to be of a *historic nature*; perhaps, of a divine "affirmation" within the Hispanic community.

The Christening

"Columbus sailed the ocean blue In fourteen hundred and ninety-two."

*W*e in America are quick to embrace her course and causes, polices and laws, quick to echo the hearts of those of the recent past: *"America...love it or leave it!"* For are we proud to be known as Americans—trumpeting our own unique heritage, institutions, a diverse people heralding *unity, freedom, equality*, and *justice.* As our "American culture" has given much for which are we thankful. Those amongst us who *share* a memory of a *bygone era*, may call to mind a painterly presentation of a *Thanksgiving* feast by *America's* premiere painter and illustrator *Norman Rockwell.* The body of family members seated about *Thanksgiving mass*, shares a spirit of "oneness" and "thanks"...thus receiving *Grace* and "freedom from want." This is our America. Yet, as with all things, America has a beginning.

We think of the "forging" of America with the onset of this now national tradition *of* a body of *101* colonists-the first permanent *English* settlement in the "New World" (in *North America*), in the year *1620.* Some thirty-five of this body's members were *Puritans* escaping "religious persecution." Thus did the *Mayflower* bore this body *freely* upon these shores.

The winter elements took their toll upon this body, however, reducing the number considerably.

Still, this body survived—with the helpful body of neighboring Indians. These two dissimilar cultures assembled...coming together as *one* body "in thanksgiving." Thus, was born the "first" Thanksgiving. However, this "spirit" was not to last.

For the antipathetic to this "prayerful" first beginning, the first body of *Black souls* to broach the American shores (in *Jamestown, Virginia*, in the year 1619) did so not freely, but as "chattel"— slaves whose primary course it was to give service to man...not GOD. In crept the institution of slavery.

First, was there introduced the practice of "indentured servitude." These souls, white and otherwise, were encouraged to barter away their freedom for a length of five to seven years, becoming the servant of the "patron" standing the cost of "passage" to the New World. In time, however, disenchanted white "servants" would "break" their compact by running away and blending into his in-kind surroundings. This did not help to maintain a stable economy; thus the gracious participants during that first thanksgiving—the American Indians—were lashed to the yoke...and were thus decimated in number. Their "spirit" did not "agree" with enslavement. Thus was a new, different source of labor required.

Through and through the "passage" they were borne. This "Middle Passage" crossed many a dark soul from homeland Africa to the beginnings of a new, alien world. All dark culture, targeted, was stripped where possible and a shining new, "unifying" symbol was lashed upon the backs of these newly misfortune souls. From the condition of cultural independence were they "delivered," royal and common, unto bondage of a common cross for an alien common good.

Their cross, Christianity, the common good, slavery operated in tandem—providing food, shelter, clothing that they themselves were responsible for growing, building, and maintaining. Under this institutionalized system was "religion" tolerated only in a controlling, manipulative fashion. Education was, however, outlawed. And family units were allowed in name only. Black souls, whether born into slavery or sold into this condition, were deemed bondsmen in perpetuity. Flourished thus slavery; flourished thus America.

Even so, yet were these dark souls not absent from memory, as souls dark in grief upon the shores of Africa promised unto themselves the returning of their missing loved ones. Perhaps, it is these continual remembrances that aided those stranded upon the shores of distant America to recall and to cling tightly to their own personal, secreted beliefs—the spiritual and the mischievous—the shamanism and the "joker."

Today's American children may recall tales by Joel Chandler Harris, tales of Bro' Rabbit and Bro' Tar Baby—tales borrowed from the telling tails of this "snatched up" and yoked body of souls; tales that kept the coals banked during such troubling times; tales that fired hotly the imaginations of these misfortune ones. For, though these dark souls were yoked to an institution of slavery, their embracing of their cross, Christianity, did not enslave their will nor hinder their creativeness. In stead of becoming a burden for this dispossessed group, Christianity became a "window" to the "thoughts" and concerns of the Creator. For these souls shackled, no "masterful" lie could strip away the truth revealed in the Black preachers at pontification, as intoned in the creations of Black "spirituals"—hope, solace, deliverance.

Still, did the "joker" remain a part of the personality of this disenfranchised folk. As the poem "The Christening" suggests, craft and ingenuity became steadfast exercises in their survival.

Affrikata

There has been a "relationship" unkind between America and the  rest of the world. We have witnessed from the comfort of our living rooms the slaughter of 800,000 Africans (the majority being Christians) in the area of Rowanda…as the pontiffs debate as to the range of the following day's numbered dead. Likewise, in the area of Herzegovina did U.S. leaders allow the decimation of a Moslem culture and people—a people with which the US shared a compact, no unlike that shared with Israel.

Yet, is there still more. We showed little interest in the flooded regions of Mozambique, while dark souls stranded on rooftops and treetops were being swept away with rising tide and day upon day exhaustion—as our leaders attempted to "seduce" the Russian leadership in allowing the U.S. to "rescue" their *Kursk*'s (submarine) dead. Nor did we barely blink an eye as *News* accounts parade before our eyes the outright slaughter by Israeli army militia of Palestine children—within their own borders—for merely tossing stones…while our leaders "encourage" no ill thought towards the slayers. Truly, "unkind" has been our relationship with the rest of the World.

But, soon come a "spirit" that permeates…even during the days of Blessed thanks and giving. The Black community, as does *"America proper,"* wraps itself in celebration during *holy* times of "love" with "giving." It is at such times that one may recall the image of the flighted *dove* returning to Noah with an *olive branch* between his beak…during the days of the deluge; or bring to mind, one may, an image of *Christ* "at baptizing," having a *dove* to descend from the heavens and the *"Heavenly Father"* affirming the "deed" and "doings" of *Christ* and the *"Baptist"*—affirming such to *His own* liking.

Still, come on that "spirit" that permeates…bitter, alien to the soul of the American ideal. What of this troubling thought…this alien "spirit"?

The *"mystery"* is wrapped up in the "presence of day." Consider this thought: since George W. Bush professes to speak with his *God*, what might one "divine" from his pronouncement? One may recall his "proclamation." While preparing for America's "Day of Independence"—the *Fourth of July*—George W. Bush proclaims that he *himself* shall "shoot" the *doves;* he *himself* shall "barbeque" the *doves;* he *himself* shall "eat" the *doves!*

The poem "Affrikata" was "born" before the "seat of power" in America "exchanged" hands. Not only does the poem "weigh" a "change" and its pending, global effect; but as the World beyond the world of America's Black community appears very recently cleaved asunder, this poem seems to bespeak the "issuing in" of this now global present-day "spirit."

Gifting

Parentage is not an activity borne by a single individual. There are 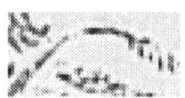 needs on all sides, on the part of mother, father and child. In attendance with these needs come implied "rights." This thought is the declaration of the poem, "Gifting." However, there is a "linked" thought not so pronounced, but just as meaningful that allows for decision making. This thought second is as much a part of the Black community as in America proper. This "link," if engaged, means termination—abortion.

In the beginning was America caught up in the need, the desire to provide relief for that number of women, who by one reason or other (via incest, rape, or delicate health), could not bear up under the strictures of childbirth and/or nurturance.

Not being our own Creator, yet was born by the concerned a law, policy, program that would allow "lawful" termination of life only for those most dire circumstances—and, perhaps, that situation whereas the unborn's own form and health may be in question. Conversely, what had been instituted as a measured embrace of compassion, has been replaced with an ever widening floodgate outside the perimeter of "original intent."

Thus, where compassion had been a ruling factor in the determination of need, now was it replaced with this ideal: "the right of woman to govern her own body." Whereas initial intent regarded the unborn as human, now was she considered but as some non discerning glob of matter—nothing more. No relation to human life nor rights regarding human life need be considered.

Presently is there compassion reserved…for the female only. How far from the celebration of life, the counting of fingers and toes, the motherly embrace has this purpose drifted. Presently may the unborn be "carried" up to a point, only to be "induced" into life, then terminated—whole and complete—so that the "would-be" mother may grieve, experience "closure" and get on with her own "rites," "privileges," and "designed" life…*precious.*

There is no argument that can relegate human life to that of questionable human life. The turtle issues forth from the turtle egg, the chick from the chicken egg, the child…the human. This has been long established as scientific fact. Also, no life goes unconfirmed; all human life is affirmed, and precious. Let's not make the "automatic" right of the one the automatic denying of rights to others.

No person has the "right" to disband the life of the innocent. Concerning decision making involving a dire circumstance, no one person should have the sole burden or duty in determining the termination of any human life.

One may appreciate the woman's "right" to conceive or not to conceive. Still, a relationship between man and woman only enhances the man's role, his involvement during conception of the unborn. This relationship between man and woman can be better appreciated if one adopted the *Biblical* view that "the body of the man belongs to the wife, and the body of the woman belongs to the husband." Why is it then that the "option" of *life* or *death* is placed solely in the "rights" column of the woman; that the man is legally stripped of rights in this one circumstance? Otherwise, is he held to some portion of responsibility.

If life is a "gift" from *God,* who has a *true* right to have the unborn terminated? If man's *God* can know the individual even before he is born, then how can the integrity of the unborn be in question? If man is not his own Creator, then what right has he to destroy a gift of creation?

Therefore, should one question himself about the "rights" of his neighbor, of his family members, of his own, he is free to answer: "All rights have an equal cause for existing. A woman has a right to her body; a wife has a right to her husband; a father has a right to his child; and a child has a right to be born. The all-encompassing question should not be about who holds the right to terminate life, but more in line with the poem, it should be about nurturing, building memories the unborn, now born may treasure up.

Mr. Chapman

Elements of "class struggle" and isolation permeate this poem—  American or no. "Design" has cleaved a gulf between the two classes. Yet, is it by God's hand or man's. If *God* has appointed governments as *charge d'affairs* over the affairs of men—and has, in deed, "ordained" them as *legal* and, perhaps, *moral* "lights"—to direct such earthly affairs...and moral temperance, then what might "countrymen" expect from their guardians; how might men respond?

America's forefathers sought to design a broad based governing power with "checks and balances" that should *guarantee* and *secure* the rights and privileges of the American people—and all within her borders.

Historically, however, governments have been known to "hammer" the *ant* and "pet" the *gorilla*. Thus, an evidential measuring element may be necessary. The best measuring rule for a receptive, responsive government is that of "trying times." When circumstances become difficult for its citizenry, does the government "feel their pain"?

Conversely, is there set in place a "Rule of law" that *automatically* gives the "ruling body" a pay increase, yet conversely drags its citizenry (paining for relief) through weeks—months—of debating, heaping up contention and divisiveness in the stalling of an across-the-board "cost of living increase" at the rate of three dollars over the span of two long years.

How is it that the ruling body *secures* for itself pensions and "perks," benefits of health and home maintenance, as the American "middle class" continues to "shrink"; as America's "fixed income" population (the aging and the poor) must depend on the charitable, giving heart of the citizenry or fall victim to neglect? How is it that the ruling body welcomes always itself to the "well" to be refreshed, to the "horn of plenty" to stock up to over filling it personal pantry, while these same leaders during *trying times* "encourage" the rest of America to tighten its belt—and be American enough to *sacrifice*?

Does this type of response appear beneficial to its citizenry? Does it suggest a receptiveness to a divine appointment? Here in America are we familiar with the "popular" thought of "the haves and the have-nots." For the majority of us, this thought is directed toward that little admitted to "class system"—yes, in the land of freedom and equality. Yet, it is evident (*Biblical* or otherwise) that leadership *dictates* and *controls* the immediacy and the availability of life in all cultures. If there appears to be an influenza of "haves and have-nots" at present, one can only assume that it "trickled down" from America's top, leading positions.

However, when "trickle down" is no longer an anomaly but "policy," first are privileges removed, following next are the "rights." And the populace, as in the case of Mr. Capman, is left frustrated, isolated, and denied. A response, an expectancy is not a course to ignore, deny, nor "lock away" as a *sacrifice.* What should the individual expect from its governing body, how should the citizenry respond? America has provided for her people— and all within her borders—the *Constitution.*

Expect a "living" Constitution. And keep and protect its right to breathe life continuous.

Man's free will molds the existence of man. And as it is thus demonstrated, the free will of man can and must not be construed as man doing the purpose of God—the Will of God. Too often man presses his own purpose, insisting that his deeds are one of benevolence.

Free will also extends to the collective governing body. Yet, how might a government represent its people? Please, consider the following...

In the House of representatives...a lone descending vote is cast against the general call: "by all means *and* any means necessary" resolution—this our lawmakers' response to the September 11 (2001—NY.) Assault upon American soil.

Here *must* Democratic Representative Barbara Lee (California) be commended for her sterling quality of unwavering integrity. Alone did she stand amongst a tidal wave of passions while assuring the "body," her colleagues, that she, too, understands the horror; that she, as well, wares the mantle in sharing in America's grief...loss.

This singular act of heroism and integrity has been witnessed at an earlier point in America's history. Then did Dr. Lyman Hall lend his presence before the Continental Congress when his state had elected *not* to be present—and taking with his rallying note for independence from Great Britain a "descending tone" against any modicum of institutional slavery and its "pretext" at preserving unity. This "willful" decision of Dr. Hall not only went contrary to the wishes of his state of Georgia but also the desires of the many unlike minds of the South. Yet, the consciences of Dr. Hall would only allow his "vote" to be one of integrity, and cast for the good of the body—the American people.

As in the case of Dr. Hall, does Representative Lee prove herself to be a true servant of her country. For, in all cases are the American people to be represented with utmost integrity. Will integrity produce a palatable fruit, as "good" is proved within the purpose of God.

Yet, if the "fruitage" is paining devastation, one is safe to assume that the act was one of free will—not God purposed...and far removed from the Will of God.

END NOTE
VII

Mitchell Alexander Jackson

*T*he preceding reference does not presume to supply the answer to all the *ills* of the world, nor, in deed, America's. However, by utilizing the "time honored" paradigm, "Do unto others as you would have them do unto you," this "active" approach towards another—will, with certainty, go a great distance in rectifying world and community, facilitating an encouragement of hope towards the *American dream*—and a worldwide positive result.

Can it be coincidental that the relationship of the American Black population with America's "dominant culture" mirrors the bonds between the Abrahamic brothers—the Arab and the Jew? Both are deserving of the blessings of the father—the promise having been given as to "preservation" and "abundance," not that of destitution, destruction and annihilation. Then was God's Mind centered during the ages—and is now so centered. The Mind of God is fixed upon the "Godly" purpose, not "manly" rhetoric and "back room" politicking.

Least we forget, let "deed" exemplify ourselves as Americans, or else the heart of the world and that of the individual shall feel the need to ask the question presently being presented for your assessment: If America is the New World of "promise," the "promised land," the land of opportunity holding "promise" for her populace, why then is one part of her citizenry to be guaranteed "full and immediate rights" while another sector of her population is to be "encouraged" upon *waiting* only? Perhaps, there is some disconcerting "spirit" at work to "erase" the Mind of God.

Thus, let us consider again the "Golden Rule." Let us inculcate this adage, this "saying" into "doing." Towards "mutual concerns" can its practice only define "positive fruitage." This *enacting* is not unlike the actions of the

"*Good Samaritan.*" One may venture as far to say that this "dovetails" well with the *Biblical* encouragement to "*Love thy neighbor as thy self.*"

Upon an age, it may be recalled when America was not far removed from this "active" thought through such international diplomats as Dr. Ralph Bunche. The Black statesman summed up the nature of this "spirit" when he stated that he held a personal "bias" for equality...a "bias" for peace. In the past did this "spirit" give a voice to those (Arab and Israeli) desiring to be head, desiring to be held in common.

Still, not all is rescinded to the past. For the present-day voice of Dr. Maya Angelou (under the ensign of the late Dr. King) continues to encourage America with like spirit. As late as the1993 inaugural of former President Clinton, her poetic presentation of "On Pulse Of Morning" urges America to embrace unity. Upon her urging is America to embrace *inclusion* and *tolerance.* Dr. Angelou's further insistence culminates with the need to take up "again the American Dream."

Dr. Angelou and the now near-mythical Dr. King are both wrapped up in a "presence" of greatness. And certainly, these pages make reference to the "coming forth" of a "Moses" during "dark hours" of direst need. Such is the instance in every community, be it white, Indian, or any other; no community goes without God's expression of hope...of concern.

In all cases—positive or nonplus—must there be assured "rights," "freedom," and "equality." Reassuring it is to know that where there is fostered "mutual respect," is there room for hope. Where there is hope, is there ever room for heartfelt peace and mutual prosperity. Yet, concern...caring *must* begin with the individual. In concert with his endeavors, *must* governmental bodies affirm and maintain the *individual's* rights and equity upon every level—cultural, religious, economic, educational, thereby addressing all levels—as the individual himself *must* respect and feel "honor-bound" to encourage such various differences reflecting the "American fabric." And though America is a diverse body of needs, concerns, desires, and possibilities, the *American Dream* is a "reality" deserving of all. Thus, let us all unite under that one banner—unified, complete—a partaker of the *American Dream.*

The SHORN SHARER
Thank you—m.a.j

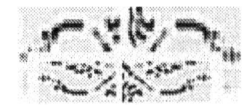

About the Author

When I was growing up in the South, it was life as usual. A fellow went through the routine of getting an education, joining the Service, possibly attaining some semblance of a higher education, but most importantly, selecting a vocation.

So, from public education, I joined the Army. This was during the Viet Nam era. Throughout my tour of duty, I hauled about my portable typewriter, my guitar, and my paints. Should a person surmise from this listing that I had a personal interest in writing, music, and art, he or she would be correct.

Yes, when growing up in the South, and following the routine, I managed to lock in the first two items on the list— "education" and "duty of service to country." Yet, vocation was a "horse of a different color." Although I cherished my love for the guitar and the *Beatles*, I set aside my music interest. Also had I interests in writing and art, from which I chose art upon which to manage a *vocation*.

But what of *vocation*—what shall it to be?

Of course, in my neighborhood, the South, vocation meant "service to man," or, on a higher level, "service to God." The impetus for work, striving, places the emphasis for doing upon the needs of another—not upon *self*. I chose to *teach*.

This choice, of course, meant attaining higher knowledge. It meant preparation of a special type, meant securing certificates and licenses. Knowing this, I strove to do acquire the necessary items and experiences. As things developed, first would I become an art teacher; later requiring ever higher learning. Thus would I become an art/English teacher—with credentials in reading. In each case, was ever the middle school my heart of hearts. Yet, it would not last.

Again was I made to consider—and to reconsider. I left my teaching position, then back to higher education—this time it was something of which I wanted no part. This was the course of the divinity—a theological program in Atlanta, Georgia. Unto this way did I apply self and soul, but my spirit longed for my "heart of hearts." I left. I left to reclaim my art, my writing, and my music.

Presently, am I soaking up the "flavors" of the West, residing in eastern Wyoming, in the historic city of Sheridan —the through way for east coast to west coast. Perhaps, one may go in either direction, if this is the suggestion. For, presently, matters within our American borders are in need of attending to. Presently, have my soul become confounded by the "spirit" in America allowing the death and dying about the world to be redressed with a footnote only. Presently, has this spirit locked up the ballot box and struck links of constriction upon the rights of the American people and upon the glory of America—a glory *true* Americans had garnered in our behalf, had placed tenderly in our keeping. Presently, perhaps, the S*pirit,* leading from the Divine, has returned. Thus, presently, have I addressed this *Spirit* and a select number of America's concerns relating to Black American aspirations within the writings of *SHORN SHARER.*